R O C K

Jam Trax

F O R   G U I T A R

by Ralph Agresta

C000154104

The original just got better!
Full-band backup to 12 extended jams in authentic
rock styles. Includes tips on scales and techniques to use
with each track. In standard notation and tablature.

Cover instruments owned by Scot Arch
Photographed by William H. Draffen
The Washburn guitar appears courtesy of Washburn International

Order No. AM 943129
US International Standard Book Number: 0.8256.1607.7
UK International Standard Book Number: 0.7119.6476.9

Exclusive Distributors:
Music Sales Corporation
257 Park Avenue South, New York, NY 10010 USA
Music Sales Limited
8/9 Frith Street, London W1V 5TZ England
Music Sales Pty. Limited
120 Rothschild Street, Rosebery, Sydney, NSW 2018, Australia

Printed in the United States of America by
Vicks Lithograph and Printing Corporation

Amsco Publications
New York/London/Sydney

CD Track Listing

1. Tuning
2. I IV V Rock
3. Home Sweet Home
4. The Bo Diddley Rhythm
5. Generation Variation
6. Honky Tonk Groove
7. Power Chords and Fifths
8. Manic Inspiration
9. Eighth-Note Riff and Power Chords
10. Syncopated Riffs
11. Heavy Rock Ballad
12. Three Fast Riffs
13. An Irresistable Beat

Table of Contents

Introduction

A couple of musician friends and I had a hard rock jam the other night and we left room for *you* to play the solos!

Hi! I'm Ralph Agresta. Join Chris Carroll (drums), John Abbey (bass), and me as we cover twelve styles commonly found in hard rock music.

The idea is to provide the beginning or advanced player with a "live" backup band for practicing solo ideas and techniques.

I've also provided a few scales and riffs for the beginning and intermediate players. Advanced players can skip right to the CD and jam along. Remember: All you have to do is follow the simple song charts provided and make up your own solos.

In some of the charts I've also included riff samples and some indication of what I've played. Non-readers should *not* panic! You don't *have* to play like me. Again, you're the soloist.

This is a great practice tool, and, as always, there is no substitute for practice.

Good luck and I sincerely hope you enjoy this book and CD and learn a great deal from them.

I IV V Rock

Pattern 1: A pentatonic

Try using this A pentatonic or blues scale.

Pattern 2: A pentatonic with pickup note and extension

This variation of the blues scale in the key of A features a pickup note, G, and extends three notes into the next octave.

Pattern 3: A major pentatonic with extension

Here are two patterns for the A major pentatonic scale.

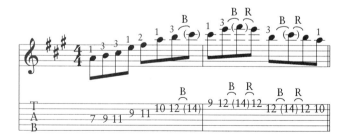

Pattern 4: A major pentatonic

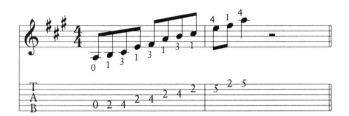

I IV V Rock

This first piece is a typical blues-based chord progression similar to Led Zeppelin's "Rock and Roll." Here, heavy guitar and drum sounds are used to turn this widely-used chord progression into a good hard rock backing track.

Riff Sample

Here's a sample of the riff I played on the backing track.

"Home Sweet Home" Country Rock

Pattern 1: A major

Here's a two-octave major scale.

Pattern 2: A major-pentatonic/major

It's common to simplify the lower octave by eliminating the fourth and seventh degree notes and to refinger the previous scale this way.

Pattern 3: A major riff

Here's a simple yet important country riff that incorporates the minor and major third.

Pattern 4: A major

Let's not forget this form of the A major scale.

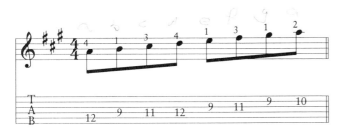

Home Sweet Home

You might think of Lynyrd Skynyrd when you hear this one. Let me suggest that you stick with major scales and riffs to create an appropriate country rock flavor.

Of course, you can use the two major-mode patterns seen in "I IV V Rock" and then combine these variations. Remember that it's not necessary for you to read the parts that I played. Just follow the basic chord changes and solo over them.

Riff Sample

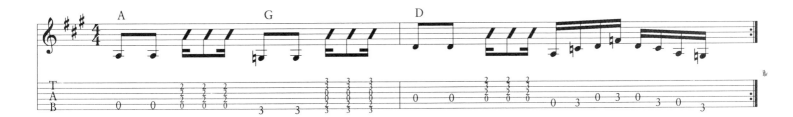

Form: [A] 1 time   [B] 9 times   [C] 8 times   [B] 7 times   [D] 1 time

The Bo Diddley Rhythm

Pattern 1: G pentatonic

Here is the obligatory G pentatonic scale.

Pattern 2: G pentatonic with passing tones

We've added to this two-octave blues scale a flatted fifth to the lower octave and a major third to the higher octave.

Pattern 3: G major pentatonic

This major pentatonic pattern will work nicely.

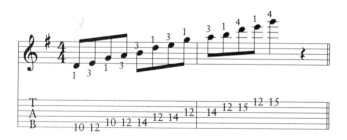

Pattern 4: G major pentatonic

This major pentatonic pattern will work nicely as well.

The Bo Diddley Rhythm

Variations of the Bo Diddley rhythm (featured here) have been used by everyone from the Who ("Magic Bus") to George Thorogood ("Who Do You Love?"). A combination of major and pentatonic scales will work nicely here.

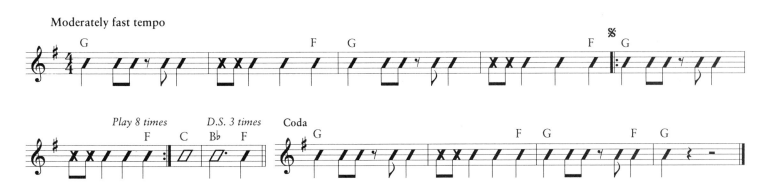

Generation Variation

Pattern 1: B pentatonic

Pattern 2: F# pentatonic

Pattern 3: B pentatonic with extension

This B pentatonic (blues) scale is repositioned and refingered. Notice in the second bar the extension with a flatted fifth.

Patterns 4 & 5: B and F# pulloff riffs

The next two patterns contain pulloff riffs that will work over the B and F-sharp chords.

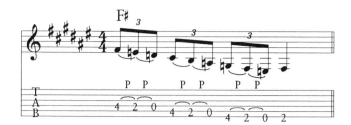

Pattern 6: B and F♯ pulloff riffs combined

For this pattern, the two previous riffs are combined for a smooth transition between the B and F-sharp chords.

Generation Variation

Who fans should have a ball with this one. Notice that although F♯ is the V chord in the key of B, it may also be treated as a transition chord, where all B major and B pentatonic scales are shifted accordingly. The first two scale patterns provide a good example.

Play 3 times

Form: A 4 times   B 2 times   A 2 times   B 2 times   A 2 times   C 4 times   Coda

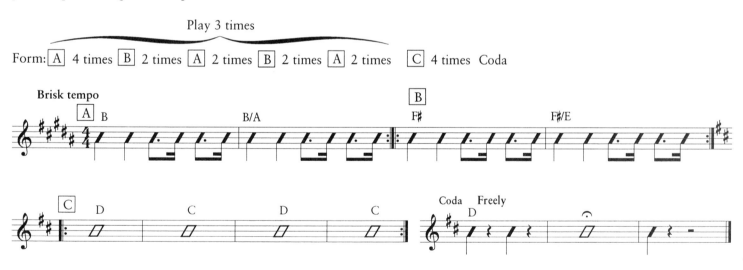

Honky Tonk Groove

For "Honky Tonk Groove," you might want to use these double-stop (two-note chord) riffs. These come straight from Chuck Berry's bag of tricks, and they work beautifully in this Rolling Stones/Rod Stewart style of music.

Riff 1

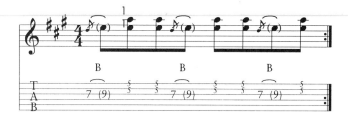

Riff 2

Riff 3

Riff 4

Honky Tonk Groove

All of the scales and patterns used for "I IV V Rock" and "Home Sweet Home" can be used here.

Remember: Don't get into a rut by practicing single-note solos only. Try playing a second rhythm part for a few of these choruses.

Power Chords and Fifths

Riff 1

Here's a riff in G that uses just the third string. It should trigger a few fresh ideas.

Pattern 1: G pentatonic

Add a fifth, sixth, ninth, and sharped- ninth to this G-pentatonic scale and you have a nice bluesy pattern.

Pattern 2: D pentatonic with bends

We've added some bends to this D pentatonic pattern.

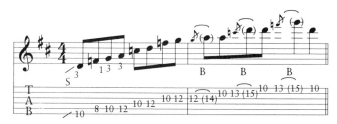

Power Chords and Fifths

This tribute to Foreigner consists of two sections: "power chords" in G and "fifths" in D.

Form: A & B 3 times; C 4 times; Coda

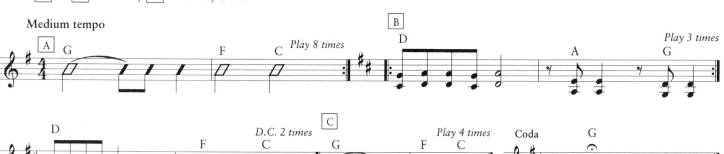

Manic Inspiration

Riff 1

Here's a riff featuring hammerons and pulloffs.

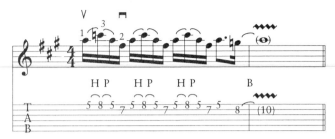

Riff 2

Watch your fingering carefully for this pattern! All of the slides should be done with the second finger.

Riff 3

Check out these A minor arpeggios.

Manic Inspiration

This one is a tribute to the master, Jimi Hendrix. "Manic Inspiration" consists of three riffs all played over an implied A chord. This really gives you great harmonic freedom; just about anything goes! This is a good track to stretch out and experiment with some new ideas.

Eighth-Note Riff and Power Chords

Pattern 1: A minor

Eighth-Note Riff and Power Chords

Shades of Bon Jovi! This one is in A minor. Try a combination of pentatonic
and minor scales.

Form: A 2 times B 8 times A 3 times C 1 time B 8 times A 3 times C 1 time B 3 times Coda

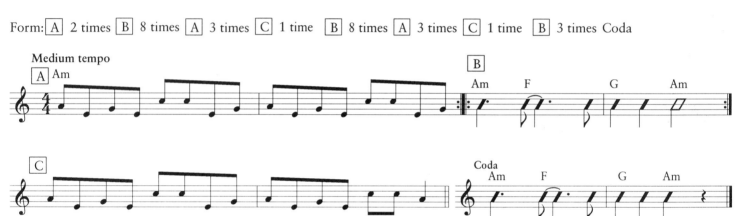

Syncopated Riffs

Pattern 1: D major

Pattern 2: D pentatonic

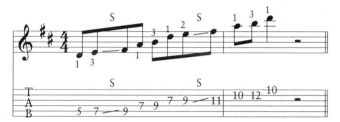

Syncopated Riffs

This piece combines two syncopated riffs in the styles of Jethro Tull and Van Halen. Remember that we looked at the F-sharp pentatonic scale in "Generation Variation." Try these D major scales and riffs for playing over the second syncopated riff.

Form: [A] 6 times [B] 4 times [A] 6 times [B] 4 times [A] 4 times Coda

Heavy Rock Ballad

Pattern 1: A minor

Here's another two-octave A minor scale.

Pattern 2: A minor

This repositioned A minor scale contains a little twist in the second octave.

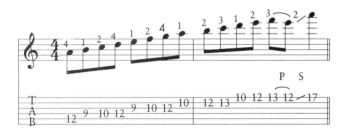

Riff 1: F major seventh and A minor scale

This riff combines an F major seventh appreggio and an A minor scale run.

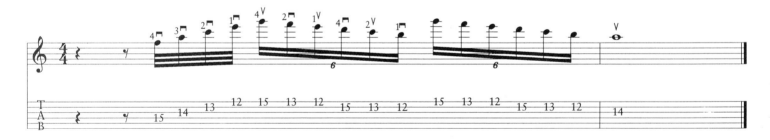

Heavy Rock Ballad

Bands like Winger, Journey, and Mountain come to mind when you hear this track. Remember that when the chord progression resolves to the A chord, you can slip into the key of A major for a measure.

Form: Drum Intro  4 times

           B 2 times (first and second ending)

           A 4 times

           B 2 times (first and second ending)

           A 4 times

           B 4 times (first ending only througout) (ritard. fourth time)

           Coda

Three Fast Riffs

Pattern 1: E blues

Here's a three-octave E blues scale.

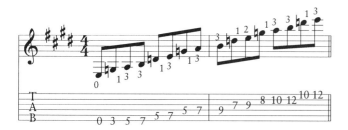

Pattern 2: E blues

This E blues scale (in the twelfth position) contains flatted fifths.

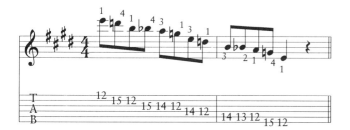

Pattern 3: E chromatic

This chromatic, hammeron riff offers a relatively easy technique for fast playing. Notice how only the first note in each set of three notes is picked. Hammer on the second and third note of each set with your second and third fingers.

Pattern 4: E chromatic

Here we see a similar technique but with a different selection of notes and, more importantly, a different rhythmic approach.

Three Fast Riffs

You'd better make sure you're warmed up for this one; some players may find it tough to keep up (sixteenth notes get pretty quick at this tempo). I had a lot of fun with this exercise, but you may find that the real challenge is to avoid sounding repetitive.

When playing over the B chord, slide the twelfth- position patterns into the seventh position, and the tenth-position pattern into the fifth position.

Play 3 times

Form: Synth and Drum Intro (not notated) A 4 times   B 4 times   C 12 times

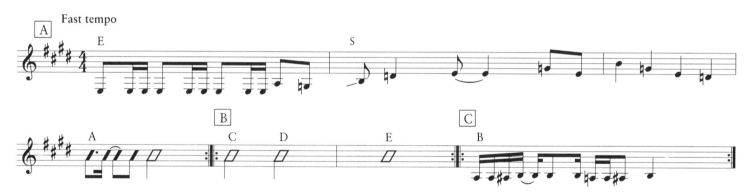

An Irresistible Beat

Finally, we return to a straight $\frac{4}{4}$ groove in the key of D. For section B, you can shift into the key of A to play over the A and C chords.

One last note for beginners: Most of the scales and riffs seen throughout this book are called moveable scales or patterns. This means that you can slide the note pattern up or down the neck to change the key of that pattern. Try this by changing the riffs and scales in E (see "Three Fast Riffs") to D simply by playing the E scale down one whole step (or down two frets).

Form: Drum intro A 4 times B 1 time A 7 times B 1 time A 4 times B 1 time A 4 times Coda

Moderately fast tempo

Drum Intro

A

S D C D C S D C D F S G F G F

S G F G C S A

C

A

C S

Coda S D C D